MW01617936

WHEN YOUR COOKIE CRUMBLES

ILLUSTRATED AND WRITTEN BY
RACHEL HOWARD

ISBN: 978-1-59849-274-3
Library of Congress Control Number: 2019915012

Printed in the United States of America

Editor: Danielle Harvey
Author Photograph: Crystal Kennedy
Design: Soundview Design

www.whenyourcookiecrumbles.com

Peanut Butter Publishing
943 NE Boat Street
Seattle, Washington 98105
206-860-4900
www.peanutbutterpublishing.com

To Emma and Clint.
May I always be your trusted baker.

Baking cookies with my mom,
she looked at me and said,

"Cookies fill your tummy, and your appetite is fed.

However, did you know they're also like your head?"

Puzzled, I asked, “How?”
She smiled, and
then she said...

"The makings of a cookie vary through and through.

Just like the ingredients that make up what is you.

Some chips remain unseen,
but forget them we must not.

Just like the emotions that are difficult to spot.

Much like feeling happiness
is similar to glee,

sadness may be murky, like
the chips we cannot see.

Deep within our cookie, there are hidden chips to seek.

Oftentimes neglected, of them we should still speak.

Laughter, joy, and happiness are important to the mix.

But anger, fear, and sadness are ingredients we cannot miss.

The butter has been added, and the chips should bake right through.

They're just like rising challenges
that are often faced by you.

But if left unattended, and your cookie shrinks in size,

with attention, care, and kindness,
you will see your cookie rise.

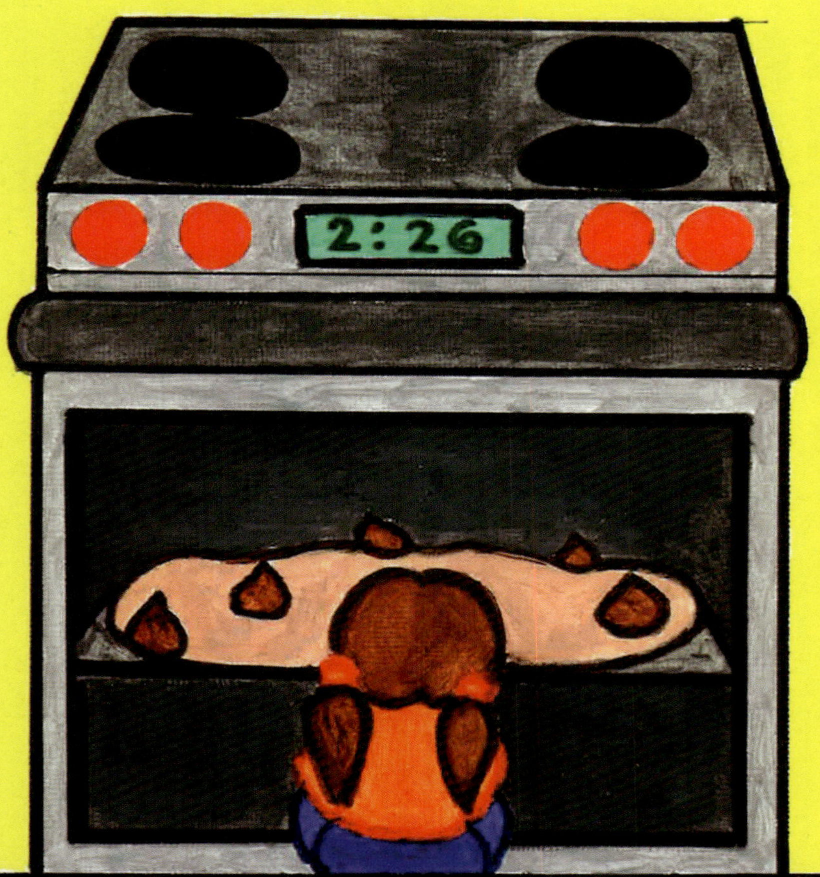

Or when your cookie crumbles and scatters on the floor, unsure just what you need to do, it hurts you at your core.

Cleaning up the little crumbs
may put you to the test.

But a cookie's still a cookie, regardless of the mess.

Whether you are crumbling or holding strong, through and through...

Know your trusted bakers will remain kind and true.

Don't be afraid to tell me if something has made you blue.

As your cookie-maker,
I'm always here for you."

Discussion Questions

1.) In the book *When Your Cookie Crumbles,* what does the cookie represent?

2.) Why do you think that the display case on page eight pictures a variety of different types of cookies?

3.) On page eleven, the girl is wearing sunglasses and a hat. What do you think she is feeling? What do you feel are some of the emotions that are difficult to identify?

4.) What is missing on page thirteen (the chocolate chips)? The significance of this page is to reiterate that sadness is just as relevant to a person's make-up as an ingredient is to a recipe.

5.) What is the girl doing on page fifteen? What is the significance of the diary? Sometimes there are emotions that are difficult to talk about. A diary is a very useful tool to work out a person's thoughts and feelings.

6.) How is the girl feeling on page seventeen? Why?

7.) What is the "challenge" that the girl is facing on page nineteen?

8.) What is the significance of the tiny cookie on page twenty?

9.) Why did the cookie become so big on page twenty-one?

10.) What does "A cookie's still a cookie, regardless of the mess" mean?

11.) Who are the "trusted bakers"? Can you identify some of your own trusted bakers?

12.) Why is the girl's face blue on page twenty-seven? Which emotion is generally associated with the color blue? Why does she feel this way?

13.) What is the significance of the statement "As your cookie-maker, I'm always here for you"?

The "It's Okay to Crumble" Chocolate Chip Cookie

2 sticks of unsalted butter (at room temperature)
1 cup of light-brown sugar
½ cup of sugar (regular granulated white sugar)
1 teaspoon of fine pink Himalayan salt (my preference, but regular salt is fine as well)
1 ½ teaspoons of vanilla extract (my preference is a Madagascar vanilla extract)
2 eggs (I use brown eggs, as I prefer how they break)
2 ¼ cups of flour (I like King Arthur brand)
½ teaspoon of baking soda
1 ¾ cups of semi-sweet chocolate chips (Nestle brand is a trusted favorite). I have also used butterscotch chips, as my mom is a big fan. I personally find the butterscotch version much too sweet for my liking (I like my chocolate chips chilled in the fridge prior to baking).

Preheat your oven to 350°F. Combine the butter, brown sugar, and white sugar into the bowl of your electric mixer (I used the KitchenAid stand mixer with the scraper attachment). Mix on low (first setting on the mixer) until butter and sugars are evenly combined. Add your eggs one at a time with the mixer still running. Always crack your eggs into a separate dish/bowl first to avoid any shell issues. Continue mixing on the lowest setting until the eggs have been thoroughly incorporated into the sugar mixture. With the mixer still running, add the salt and the vanilla. In a separate bowl, mix your flour and baking soda together. I don't ever need to sift my flour; I just pour the dry ingredients into the wet mixture. Resume the mixer to its lowest setting until all ingredients are combined and smooth. Turn off the mixer and remove the scraper. Pour in and stir your chocolate chips until they are well combined. I use my ice-cream scooper to scoop my dough. Leave approximately one inch between each cookie on the sheet. I usually have two batches (twelve cookies per batch). Cook for fifteen minutes. You can rotate your pan if you'd like, but I do not find it necessary. When the cookies are done, remove from the hot pan immediately. You can use cooling racks, baking racks, or, like me, another baking sheet that wasn't just in the oven to let your cookies stand for a few minutes.

Some shopping tips from me to you

Ingredients can be pricy. I do believe in using quality ingredients because you really can taste the difference. Marshall's, Home Goods, or for my fellow Canadians–Winner's, more often than not carry many of the ingredients at discounted prices. I always purchase my olive oils, extracts, and Himalayan salt there. Costco sells the salt and the chocolate chips in bulk as well. Which, trust me, once you make these cookies, they are sure to become a family favorite, so buying in bulk is a good option. Enjoy!

*recipes only to be completed under the supervision of an adult

The “It’s Okay to Crumble” Chocolate Chip Cookie a la Gluten-Free Option

(for those with a gluten allergy or on a gluten-free diet)

2 sticks of unsalted butter (at room temperature)
1 cup of light brown sugar
½ cup of sugar (regular granulated white sugar)
1 teaspoon of fine pink Himalayan salt (my preference, but regular salt is fine as well)
1 ½ teaspoons of vanilla extract (my preference is a Madagascar vanilla extract)
1 tablespoon of milk (you can use any type you like; I use 2% and avoid any nut milk due to allergies)
2 eggs (I use brown eggs, as I prefer how they break)
2 ¼ cups of King Arthur’s Gluten-Free All-Purpose Baking Flour (by far the BEST gluten-free flour option)
½ teaspoon of baking soda
½ teaspoon of xanthan gum (I use Bob’s Red Mill)
1 ¾ cups of semi-sweet chocolate chips (Nestle brand is a trusted favorite). I have also used butterscotch chips, as my mom is a big fan. I personally find the butterscotch version much too sweet for my liking (I like my chocolate chips chilled in the fridge prior to baking).

Preheat your oven to 350°F. Combine the butter, brown sugar, and white sugar into the bowl of your electric mixer (I used the KitchenAid stand mixer with the scraper attachment). Mix on low (first setting on the mixer) until butter and sugars are evenly combined. Add your eggs one at a time with the mixer still running. Always crack your eggs into a separate dish/bowl first to avoid any shell issues. Continue mixing on the lowest setting until the eggs have been thoroughly incorporated into the sugar mixture. With the mixer still running, add the salt, the vanilla, and the milk. In a separate bowl, mix your flour, xanthan gum, and baking soda together. I don’t ever need to sift my flour; I just pour the dry ingredients into the wet mixture. Resume the mixer to its lowest setting until all ingredients are combined and smooth. Turn off the mixer and remove the scraper. Pour in and stir your chocolate chips until they are well combined. Let your dough sit in the mixer for about thirty-five minutes. Gluten-free baking can be tricky because of the rising element. Letting it sit for a bit will help. I use my ice-cream scooper to scoop my dough. Leave approximately one inch between cookies on the sheet. I usually have two batches (twelve cookies per batch). Cook for fifteen minutes. You can rotate your pan if you’d like, but I do not find it necessary. When the cookies are done, remove from the hot pan immediately. You can use cooling racks, baking racks, or, like me, another baking sheet that wasn’t just in the oven to let your cookies stand for a few minutes. Regardless of my technique, I generally will have at least two cookies break or crumble, leaving the chef to sample the product before serving. Enjoy!

*recipes only to be completed under the supervision of an adult

RACHEL HOWARD grew up in Windsor, Ontario. She graduated from the University of Windsor with a Bachelor of Arts in English. Upon graduating, she accepted a job overseas in South Korea, where she taught children of all ages. During that time, she had the opportunity to travel throughout Asia, spending time in Cambodia, Japan, Laos, and Thailand. *When Your Cookie Crumbles* is her first published children's book. She drew upon her own experiences as a mother in cultivating a charming, metaphoric story that delves into the vast psyche of a child and his or her emotions.

Photograph by Crystal Kennedy

She is a self-taught artist, who loves to paint and create keepsake images for her family. She enjoys cooking and trying new recipes. Most of all, she loves to bake with her children. Rachel lives in the picturesque Pacific Northwest with her husband and two children.